A Tiny Book About Price

A Tiny Book About Price

A step-by-step guide to pricing your work

by Chris Zielski

Three Leaves Press

Copyright © 2023 by Chris Zielski

All rights reserved. No parts of this book may be reproduced in any form without written permission from the author.

ISBN 978-1-7366284-3-0 *(paperback)*

Published by
Three Leaves Press
ThreeLeavesPress.com

*This book is dedicated to my husband Alan.
Thank you for being my everything.*

Table of Contents

Formulas And Flashbacks	3
Invisible Factors	7
The Three Markets	19
Market Price	31
The Price Box	53
The Value of Work	77
Strategic Pricing	85

Formulas And Flashbacks

Pricing has long been one of the most challenging aspects for creative professionals. It's tricky for a variety of reasons. When we sell things we make, we often take our time and skills for granted. We don't always know how to financially value the intangible aspects of our work. Or, we may feel uncomfortable taking money for something we inherently enjoy. And that doesn't even include figuring out how to come up with a number! But once you make the decision to sell your work, price is a critical part of the equation.

So where do you start?

(Materials + Labor + Overhead = Wholesale) x2 = Retail
x (the average speed of a train going northwest at 35km/hr)
= a giant headache + putting it off til tomorrow

There are plenty of formulas out there. But if formulas give you flashbacks to grade school story problems, you're not alone. Sure, they can lead you to a number. But if that number doesn't feel right or if you're not comfortable saying it out loud, it won't do you any good.

The purpose of this book is to help you determine your Right Price. You'll uncover the qualities that create value within your work, research your market, and calculate your costs. And, you'll approach price in a way that feels connected to who you are and what you make.

When you come to a place where you know both what your Right Price is and why, you'll feel much more confident and comfortable communicating it. Most importantly, you'll learn to see price not just as a number, but as a strategic tool to help you achieve your ultimate goal: selling your work.

This book covers pricing from three main perspectives: *tactical*, *emotional*, and *strategic*. Each chapter includes a variety of exercises to help you uncover and quantify the various factors that go into your price.

On the tactical side:

Invisible Factors helps you articulate the various attributes that create value within your work.

The Three Markets teaches about product-market alignment and the role market plays in pricing. You'll use this chapter to determine the ideal market for your product.

Market Price helps you research similar products within your market to give you a sense of pricing norms.

The Price Box balances your Market Price against your various expenses to make sure you've adequately covered your costs.

On the emotional side:

The Value of Work dives into the emotional aspects of pricing. Emotions can play a huge role in how you value your work and how comfortable you are communicating that value. You'll learn to identify and rebalance any emotional roadblocks you may have, and learn five simple tips to take the ick out of talking about money.

On the strategic side:

Strategic Pricing is all about using price as a strategic tool. You'll learn to leverage a market, attract the right buyers, and take your work and business to a whole new level.

Invisible Factors

The Tale of a Tile

When I first started working in metal, my work was a collection of playful experiments. What would a design look like etched into copper? What if I gave it this patina or that? When people started asking to buy my creations, I was forced to think about pricing.

The first pieces I sold were small tiles. I had no idea what to charge, so I priced them at $10. The metal squares I was using cost around $5 back then, so I figured $10 should be about right. I sold them happily, and didn't think much about it. I had a day job at the time, and the money I made selling them more than covered the cost of my material — at least, the only one I was counting. Wasn't it great to have a hobby that paid for itself!

As I started to share my designs, people began to take notice. A woman in the art community invited me to an outdoor show where I could sell my work. I was flattered to be asked. The show was free; all I had to do was get there early to help my host set up. And, create an enticing display. And… spend ten long hours in the blazing sun as people walked by.

Some people loved my work, and a few certainly purchased. But others made offhanded comments and tossed my work aside. At one point I stepped away and let someone else tend my stand for a moment. When I returned, I found my display on the ground. Someone had accidentally knocked it over and left without so much as an apology.

I made a bit of money at the show, certainly more than I had up to that point. But inside I felt tired and resentful. How could people be so careless with my work? Why did I help at the event for free? I had agreed to be there willingly, but afterward felt like my time and work hadn't been valued. I raised my price to $15 to convey that value.

As I made more and more tiles, I began to experiment with different techniques and new materials. I started cutting and layering my designs, doubling or tripling the amount of materials in each piece. My work became more intricate and my process more involved. I began to realize that my materials included more than just metal. There was the wood back I mounted it to, the chemistry I used to create the designs, even the box I put it in when it was finished. I raised my price to $20 to adequately cover those costs.

That summer I went to a juried art show. There was an artist selling items somewhat similar to mine. They were a different style, but roughly the same size and materials. Except that hers were $25. They were so beautiful I bought three. By the time I walked back around, she had nearly sold out. I was happy for her, and for myself as well – if she could sell her work at that price, so could I. Buyers were clearly willing to pay it. I went home and raised my price to $25.

I set aside some money and went to the same show the following year, hoping to buy a few more pieces from the same artist – but found that she had raised her price to $35. *Ouch!* I bought two instead of the three I'd planned for. And I raised my own price to $30. If her work was worth more, mine was too.

The following year, I was accepted into my own juried art show. I paid the hefty fee for the show, plus bought a canopy, some tables, and a handful of displays. It was a big investment at the time, but it gave me an opportunity to present my work to a wider audience. I raised my price to $35 to help cover the cost of my new expenses.

I opened my booth and a young man came in and admired my work. He spent a great deal of time complimenting my designs, but said "Thirty five bucks?! You must be making a *killing*!" ...and walked away empty-handed. *Sure*, I thought wryly to myself as I looked around at the hundreds of dollars' worth of stuff that made up my display. And I hadn't even sold anything yet!

A young woman walked in soon after. She carefully looked over all of my items, then selected a few pieces and handed me a folded up wad of bills. I wrapped the pieces delicately and thanked her for her purchase. The sale was simple, almost effortless. *Here,* I thought, *is my right buyer*.

Later that year, I started to sell my work through retail locations. I put my items in galleries and sold them to consignment shops. My pieces sold well, but the income was split between the shop owners and me. They each had their own expenses, just as I had mine. I looked closely at my time and materials and the percentage of each sale I would receive. I crunched some numbers and raised my price to $40.

I returned to the art show the following summer. I kept my price at $40 to keep it consistent with my retail locations. Throughout the show, I received plenty of offhanded comments – some critical and some careless – but many more quiet buyers, happily handing over their money for my work. Each time someone purchased one of my items, I thanked them gratefully. Each time someone loudly balked at my prices, I smiled and thought to myself: *You are not my buyer.*

Invisible Factors

Over time, I raised my price on those little tiles for a variety of reasons. Some increases were influenced by the cost of my materials or time. Some were impacted by how or where I sold my work. And some were a reflection of my market. At every level, my price made sense for where I was at the time. I'm not suggesting that my *methods* for setting those prices were always right – I was a beginner at one time, just like everyone. I learned and improved as I went along.

My point is this... we often think of price as a big fixed entity, etched in stone for all time. Or, that it's the answer to a complicated math problem – and if we only do the equation right, we'll be set. The truth is that price is relative, and can – and should – evolve over time. It's a reflection of a variety of factors, and those factors can change.

Does this mean that price is random or meaningless? Of course not. It's an important piece of a larger puzzle – one that includes your product, your market, your venues, and your professional goals. As the pieces of your puzzle evolve and change, so too should your price.

In my tile story, virtually every facet of my work changed over time. When I first started out, making tiles was a hobby. It gradually developed into a business over a period of several years. My items started out fun and experimental and became more planned and intricate. I increasingly invested more time and my materials grew more expensive.

My marketing and buyers changed as well. When I started selling my work, my customers were mostly people within my small circle, and I sold to them directly. As I began to sell to a wider audience, my tone grew more professional. I did more prestigious shows, had nicer displays, and sold my work through more established venues.

When we see price as a fixed number, a sum of an equation based solely on time and materials or other concrete factors, what we're really doing is not acknowledging all the less quantifiable aspects of our work. How do you calculate your market? The desirability of your product? Your level of skill? Your larger professional goals? Some of these are intangible, even intuitive. But they should be factored into your price.

The next few chapters will give you insights into these less tangible aspects so you can have a more well-rounded view of your price. Rather than just settling on a number, you'll be creating a tool that you can use to attract the right audience, connect with a particular market, convey a sense of value, create product desirability, and reach your personal and professional goals.

But first, we're going to start where pricing should always begin: *your product.*

Your Product

As creative professionals, we often think of our products in terms of nouns, but they're adjectives as well. And those adjectives can have a huge impact on price.

For example if you're a baker, you may sell *bread*. That's the noun. But if your bread is *organic, hand-milled, whole grain,* those adjectives will have as much of an impact on your price as the fact that your product is a loaf of bread.

In this section, you're going to describe your product so you can tease out those adjectives and start to quantify them.

When it comes to descriptions, there are two ways you can describe an item: *effective* and *affective*. These words may look similar, but they're very different.

An effective description is *practical*. Think physical, formal, technical. It's cut, dry, and specific. It's the nuts and bolts of your product. It usually includes things like materials, ingredients, techniques, and measurements. For example, my tile might be 4x4 inches, made of copper, mounted on a wood backing, and ready to hang on a wall.

An affective description is *emotive*. It's all about the sensory details. It's still descriptive, but in a way that appeals to your buyer's heart rather than their head. It usually includes sensory aspects like color, texture, smell, feel or taste. While an affective description doesn't have to use flowery language, it should be appealing and enticing. For example, my tile might be a rich crimson red thickly etched with a Japanese maple leaf design.

Choose one of your products to focus on throughout the next few chapters. It can be your average product, your biggest seller, or just something that represents your work in general. Focusing on a single product will help you be more targeted in your descriptions and allow you create a baseline price that can be adjusted to fit any similar products you may have – products where the noun is the same but the adjectives are different. If you have very different product lines, i.e. where the nouns are different as well, go through the exercises for each type of item.

On the following worksheet, write your product at the top of the page. This should be a simple word or two that tells what your product is, whether it's a metal tile or a loaf of bread. No elaboration here – just the noun.

In the top section, write an effective description of your product. Be practical and specific, and include things like materials, ingredients, techniques, and measurements. I often write this as a bullet list because that makes it easy to skim and gives it a more technical feel.

In the bottom section, write an affective description of your product. Remember that affective is about *appealing*. Your description should focus on sensory details that appeal to potential buyers. Use a thesaurus to help you find just the right words, or ask a friend to help you describe your product. Spend some time on this one and you'll have a great marketing blurb you can use later on.

If you get stuck on your affective description, think of what your work is not. What's the opposite of what you create? What type of item would have the same noun but vastly different adjectives?

For example, the opposite of that organic, hard-milled whole grain loaf of bread is a loaf of commercial white sandwich bread – what my daughter calls "squishy bread". Starting from the opposite end of the product spectrum may help you articulate what makes your work valuable or unique.

The purpose of this activity is to get you thinking about the less tangible aspects of your product. You'll be quantifying them later. Not only will they be crucial in helping you settle on a price, they're exactly the sort of information you'll share with potential buyers to convey the value of your work.

Save your descriptions. You'll refer back to them later.

Your Product:

_____

Effective description:

Affective description:

The Three Markets

Markets, Distilled

When I was younger, I loved to bake. The smell of cinnamon and brown sugar would fill my tiny kitchen. One of my recipes called for a teaspoon of almond extract. I bought a large jug of it, the only size I could find at the time. It led me to wonder, what is extract, anyway? The clear liquid was magically filled with fantastic aromas.

I looked it up and found out it wasn't very magical at all — it was simply almonds soaked in vodka. In fact, that's all any extract is. Vanilla, lemon, peppermint – they're all just stuff soaked in alcohol for a few weeks.

So I decided to make some.

I started with vanilla, the stalwart of any baker's arsenal. I went to the grocery store and picked out some whole vanilla beans and looked around for a bottle of vodka. I'd never bought vodka before, and wasn't sure where they kept it. But I quickly found it, nestled between the dried cranberries and the slivered almonds. I checked out, feeling very grown up – they didn't even ask for my ID.

I poured some of the vodka into pretty glass bottles and carefully added the vanilla beans. I set them on a sunny shelf and waited.

And waited.

And... waited.

Three weeks, then six, then several months went by and the liquid still looked exactly the same. I opened it up and gave it a sniff. It smelled, but not like magic.

I relayed the story to my then-boyfriend over the phone. He tried to problem-solve from a distance. "What kind of vodka did you use?" he asked. I didn't know, and the bottle was long gone. "Well... what shelf was it on?" Why, the bottom one, right next to the dried cranberries. "I think I see your problem," he said gently.

Apparently there's an entire liquor store *inside* the grocery store that I hadn't even noticed. I'd bought *baking* vodka, which was as close to a non-alcoholic beverage as I could get. No wonder it wasn't extracting. In hindsight, the price should have been a clue – the quart-sized bottle cost less than a tiny bottle of vanilla extract. And the proof was quite literally in the pudding.

Fast forward a few years, I married that patient man. We now live in the country, surrounded by farms and vineyards. One of those vineyards distills vodka from the grapes they grow. I still don't drink it, but I know without even tasting it that what they make is top of the top shelf. They have a beautiful turn-of-the-century barn and a two-story copper still. On hot summer evenings, you can smell the grapes distilling as you drive by.

Baking vodka, grocery store vodka, and copper still vodka are all technically vodka, but they're very different products. Their price point is different, their exclusivity is different, and they're used for different purposes. Baking vodka is used to add flakiness to pie crusts. It has little alcohol and available for anyone to buy – you don't even need an ID. Copper still vodka makes the finest martinis. It's so exclusive it's not even sold in stores – you have to drive out to the country to get it.

The Three Markets

All products fall loosely into one of three markets: *accessible*, *midrange*, or *exclusive*. There's nothing judgmental about these categories – one isn't any better or worse than another. They're just different. It might not make vanilla extract, but baking vodka has its place.

Your product has a place, too. You might intuitively know which market it falls into, but if you don't, read through the following statements to see which ring true (or which you want to be true) for your product:

Accessible Market:

My product is quick and easy to make.
My product is enjoyed by a wide variety of people.
Most people understand and appreciate what I make.
I want my product to be accessible and inexpensive.
I'm able to produce my product in quantity.

Midrange Market:

My product takes a bit of time and skill to create.
My skills or knowledge took time and effort to learn.
I can only make so many products due to the labor involved.
I want or need to charge a higher price due to
the level of craftsmanship involved.
While many people love what I do, not everyone "gets" it.
I want to sell my work to people who appreciate it.

Exclusive Market:

My product takes a great deal time or a high degree of expertise to make.
I am a master at my craft; few people have achieved my level of skill or knowledge.
I want my work to be exclusive or high end.
I sell to connoisseurs who truly appreciate the quality and skill involved.
I want or need to sell my work at a premium.
I recognize that not everyone will want, like, or be able to afford my work.
I'm willing to be patient and wait for just the right buyer.

Each of these markets should give you a different feeling as you read them. Think of a few products you've bought or advertisements you've seen. Which market do they each belong to? Then think of your own product. Where does it fit?

The caveat here is that you can only pick one. Each product has to fit cleanly into a single market. You can't mix and match statements from one and another. Each market attracts a particular audience –

and by default, leaves others out. A connoisseur won't be attracted to an accessible item, and someone looking for something inexpensive won't want a high end product.

Many creative professionals, myself included, make the mistake of mixing categories in the early stages of their creative careers – only to find out it doesn't work. They may spend a fair amount of time making their items, but want to keep their price low so they'll reach a wider audience – only to discover they're not fully covering their time or materials. Or they undercharge for a premium product thinking it will lead to more sales, but all it does is turn off the high-end audience they're trying to attract. Or they overcharge for a product before they have the skills or expertise to back up their high-end price.

When your product, your price, and your audience aren't in alignment, marketing and selling your work becomes much more difficult. But when they are, things click. Selling gets easier. Sure, you still have to market your work. But you know who you're trying to reach.

More importantly, you know who your audience *isn't*. So when you get a comment from a bystander that your work is too this or too that, you can quietly say to yourself: *You are not my buyer.*

The good news is that bringing your product, your price, and your audience into alignment is relatively straightforward: all you have to do is choose a market and stay there. Without wavering or blinking. Or if you must change, change *everything*. Move to a new market and embrace it.

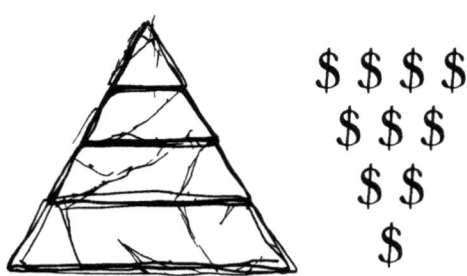

Remember, there is no judgment in choosing one market over another. You can even make the same amount of money; you'd just do it in different ways. Someone selling an accessible product would create a larger volume of goods and sell them inexpensively to a wider audience – let's say they sell 100 $10 items. Someone selling a midrange product would sell fewer items at a higher price point to fewer people – let's say they sell 10 $100 items. Someone selling an exclusive product would sell a small number of items to a tiny number of buyers who are willing to pay a premium – for example, a single $1000 item.

Take care not to mistake price for income here. All three hypothetical sellers in the previous example end up making the same amount of money; they just do it in different ways. Price is about selling your work for an appropriate amount of money to people who value it. Market consistency helps attract those people. It conveys who your product is for.

On the following worksheet, reflect on the three markets using the statements on p. 23-24 as a guide. Which market does your product belong in? Which statements ring true for your work?

Your Market:

Which market does your product belong in? Is it accessible, midrange, or exclusive? Why?

Did your product fit cleanly into a single market? If so, which one? If not, what adjustments will you need to make going forward? Making tweaks to your product or intended market at this stage will make settling on a price much easier. As you research your Market Price next, you'll have a clear view of where your work should fall within a broader context.

A side note: it is possible to offer products for more than one market, say a midrange product and an exclusive one. You just can't mix markets for the *same* product. The products themselves must be qualitatively different. I'll talk about how to tap into multiple markets and when it may make sense to do so in *Strategic Pricing: Bread And Butter*.

Market Price

House Hunting

When I got married, I sold my house in the city and my husband and I bought our farmhouse in the country. While I'd purchased a house before, selling one was a new experience for me. I didn't know the process and had no idea how to price it. I found a realtor and we talked through things together.

The realtor went through a process called *pulling comps*. Pulling comps refers to finding comparable properties that had recently sold in my area. They had the same number of bedrooms as my house, were of a similar size, and were in or near my little neighborhood. The particulars may have been different – my garage was shiny and new, but theirs had a finished basement or an extra bathroom – but overall, they were similar. The comps gave us some rough numbers to start with.

She then pulled out a few properties that were currently for sale and we did a little scrutinizing. The one down the street with the nice addition? Their price was on the higher end, but probably worth it. The one that was run down? The owner had passed away and it was priced cheap. The one in great shape with the lowest price? The couple was having a baby and wanted to move SOON. And that one that was just *meh*, but asking for the moon? Well, they could ask, but they probably wouldn't get it.

I didn't always know the backstory, but by looking at a broad spectrum of comps we could see where each individual house price fit into a bigger picture.

Because my house was in the middle of the spectrum, we settled a listing price in the middle of the most similar properties.

When my husband and I were buying our current house, we went through a similar process to make sure the asking price was fair. But the process wasn't as straightforward. We were buying an old farmhouse out in the country. There hadn't been many sales in the neighborhood because, well... there wasn't really much of a neighborhood. The other houses in the township were over a century newer, and most of the older homes were in sorry shape, unlike the well-cared for charmer we were interested in. It was hard to find anything similar in terms of age, size, condition, and location. Maybe one or two aspects would match, but not all.

So the realtor used what she could find. She pulled out houses that had sold nearby plus a few similar properties from neighboring areas.

We looked at the range and made some judgments. The highest price? It had come from a newly built mansion on a pristine piece of land. The lowest? A crumbling old house that had seen better days. The one that was the most similar? It had sold a few years back when the market was less favorable.

Because our house was unique and desirable, we put in an offer that was slightly above the asking price.

There were lots of factors that went into a selling or buying price – comps were not the only consideration. Things like what we could afford and our personal situation certainly played a part. But the comps gave us a starting point. They provided a baseline, and then we used our judgment.

Finding Your Comps

In this section, you'll determine your Market Price. Your Market Price is the price that reasonably fits what the market expects an item like yours to cost. Much like houses, there are lots of other factors that go into a selling price – we'll talk about those later. But also like houses, comps give you a starting point. They provide a baseline that you can adjust up or down to fit your product, your costs, and your personal or professional situation.

The next few exercises will guide you through the process of finding your comps. In this case, *comps* refers to items that are similar, or similar enough, to what you sell. If your products are more common, you'll look for items that are as close to yours as possible. If your work is more unique, you may have to settle for close enough. You're like the house in the country – you can still find something similar, but it might not be a perfect match.

Look for 6-10 products that are similar to yours. You can search for comps in a variety of places – online, in retail stores, at craft shows, etc. The internet makes it relatively easy to find information for most types of products, but if you *only* use the internet, be sure to use a variety of sites rather than a single selling platform, which can sometimes skew the numbers up or down. If you find it challenging to find similar items, remember that close enough is okay.

As you find your comps, jot down the item, price, venue, and a brief description. As you do this, remember the two ways you described your own product: *effective* and *affective*. Include both straightforward details as well as sensory aspects.

The process of searching for, collecting, and describing your comps may take time, but the information you glean will be well worth the effort. You'll use it in the next few exercises to determine your Right Price.

Finding Your Comps:

Look for 6-10 products that are similar to your own. You can look online, in retail stores, at craft shows, etc. Type of venue and location can have an impact on price, so include a variety if possible.

As you find these items, note the price, type of venue, and a brief description. Include both practical and emotive aspects.

If you can't find items that are similar to your product, remember that close enough is okay!

Comp #1: _____ Price: _____
Venue: _____
Description:

Comp #2: _____ Price: _____
Venue: _____
Description:

Comp #3: _____ Price: _____
Venue: _____
Description:

Comp #4: _____ Price: _____
Venue: _____
Description:

Comp #5: _____ Price: _____
Venue: _____
Description:

Comp #6: _____ Price: _____
Venue: _____
Description:

Comp #7: _____ Price: _____
Venue: _____
Description:

Comp #8: _____ Price: _____
Venue: _____
Description:

Comp #9: _____ Price: _____
Venue: _____
Description:

Comp #10: _____ Price: _____
Venue: _____
Description:

A Bigger Picture

Once the realtor found comps for my house, we had to make comparisons to see the bigger picture. You'll be doing the same for your comps. The purpose of the comparisons is to tease out connections between price and the various aspects of those items.

Start by looking only at the prices of your comps. Use the number line on the following page to plot them. What was the lowest price? Round that number down to the nearest round number. Write it on the far left side of the line. What was the highest price? Round that number up and place it on the right side. Use the marks on the number line to create intervals between them.

Once you have your intervals marked, place a dot where each of your comp prices falls within this spectrum.

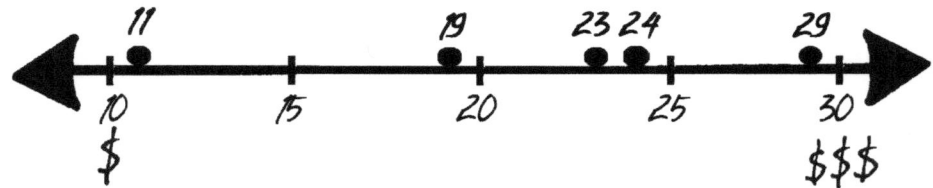

Plot Your Comps:

Use the number line below to plot the prices of your comps.

Find your lowest comp price and round it to the nearest whole number. Write it below the line on the left side. Find your highest comp price and round it to the nearest whole number. Write it below the line on the right side.

Next, use the markings on the number line to create intervals. Use $1, $5, $10, or $25 increments – whatever makes sense.

Then, plot each of your comp prices along the number line you created.

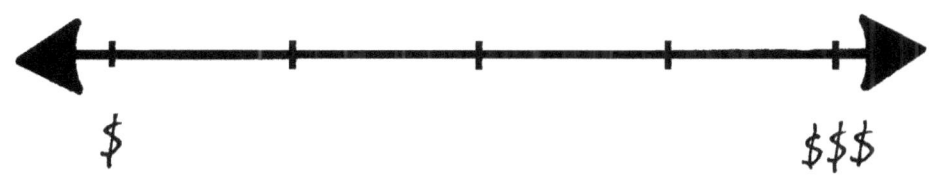

Finding Connections

Look at the numbers on your number line. Did you find a fairly consistent price range among your comps? For example, were they all in the $90-100 range? If your prices were all within say 10-15% of one another, that gives you a pretty clear picture of your market price. It doesn't mean you *have* to charge that amount, but it does give you a good baseline. If that baseline feels comfortable, you're in a great spot. If it doesn't, think about what may be giving you pause.

If your comps were all over the map (which is not uncommon, especially for art, handmade, or other creative items), then you'll have to tease out a bit more information. Start by looking for outliers. Did you have a few prices that were off the chart at either end? Look at those first.

Outliers usually occur when an item falls into a different market than the rest of your comps – think of the accessible, midrange, or exclusive markets you learned about in *The Three Markets*. Sometimes this market difference is obvious – the product is simply a higher or lower caliber than the rest of your comps. For example, that baking vodka? The price should have been a clue.

But sometimes what's causing that market difference is a bit more subtle. A single attribute can drive the price of an item much higher or lower than its peers. Let's look at some factors that may be at play.

The Five Attributes

There are five main attributes that tend to impact an item's price: *features*, *materials*, *craft*, *presentation*, and *brand*.

Let's start with some definitions.

Features are the stuff the product comes with. Is the item pretty basic or does it have a lot of extras? These extras can be part of the item itself, such as how large or complex it is, or they can be added onto the purchase – things like free delivery, frame included, etc.

Materials are what the item is made of. Is it sterling silver or 24k gold? Polyester or dupioni silk? Pine or figured maple? In many creative items, materials can have a huge impact on price – so while there may be a bit of overlap between materials and features, it's worth considering them separately.

Craft refers to the level of skill it took to make the item. Is it simple or intricate? Something the average person could make, or the work of a master? Skill can play a huge role in both the price of a product and its market.

Presentation is all about packaging. It includes the physical box the item comes in, but also things like a website if the item is sold online, the booth setup if it's sold at a craft show, or the shop display if it's sold through a physical store. These are all part of the buying experience, and can all contribute to price – even if they're not specifically part of the item. If you have trouble distinguishing between features and presentation, ask yourself if what you're reflecting on is part of the item itself, or the overall buying experience. Presentation is all about the latter.

Brand refers to name recognition. Is the artist well-known? Is the brand desirable? Is there a sense of exclusivity? Does the creator have a dedicated audience? This can be a trickier attribute to parse out, but you can usually get a sense by looking at context clues. Things like a highly polished logo, a huge social media following, or a product that sells out quickly can give you a hint. Again, there can be a bit of overlap here, but when brand plays a major role, the impact can be large.

All of these attributes can have an impact on price – and not a small one, either. Even one of these can cause a price tag to spike or fall. The same ring design made of gold instead of silver may command 100 times the price, whereas a gemstone that's really colored glass can be 1/100th. A seemingly average item that has strong brand recognition may be highly desirable – and have a price tag to match.

Look at each of your outliers to see if you can tease out which attribute is impacting its price.

Teasing Out Outliers:

Look at the outliers on your number line one at a time. Think about the Five Attributes. See if you can find connections between specific attributes and price.

Market Price

Once you've looked at your outliers and hopefully teased out a reason for their unusually high or low price point, look at the rest of your comps. Are they similar to each other in terms of attributes? Are they similar in terms of price? If not, can you find a connection between an attribute and price? Are there some that perhaps *should* be priced higher or lower when you compare them to the rest?

Do a bit of reflection, then consider your own product. Where does it fit on the spectrum? Does it fit comfortably within your comps in terms of attributes? Is it an outlier? Do you want it to be? Reflect on your product's relationship within the larger landscape.

Then settle on a price based on what you've discovered.

Market Price:

Reflect on your product in relationship to your comps. Decide on a price based on what you've discovered. Write it on the price tag below.

The number you come up with is your Market Price, as in the price that reasonably fits what the market expects an item like yours to cost. But before you put a sticker on your product, you'll want to make sure that number works for you. To do that, head to *The Price Box* next!

The Price Box

Okay, this is the part of the book where you'll have to do a little math, so grab your calculator (and maybe a martini or shot of vanilla extract) and settle in.

Imagine your price is a cardboard box – in it you put your materials, labor, and other costs. If your box is too small, your costs won't fit. If it's too big, it may be more than your customer wants to carry. The ideal scenario is to get it just right.

In this chapter, you're going to work backward by measuring your Market Price against your *materials, labor, overhead,* and *venue.*

Your Market Price is important because it gives you a sense of how big your customer expects your Price Box to be. It's called your *market* price because it reflects your market. But, you'll want to make sure this number adequately covers your time and expenses.

Materials

To calculate your materials costs, list the various materials that go into your product. As you do this, be sure to include *all* of your materials, not just the obvious ones. Hold your item in your hand. What goes into making it? Describe the steps out loud and write down each of the materials you use throughout the process. What supplies are involved that don't end up in the finished product but are expended along the way? What costs are involved in packaging and selling the item? Write them down.

If your items are small, materials costs may be easier to quantify in batches, for example by estimating your costs for 10 or 20 items versus just one. That way you're not trying to split the price of a tube of paint or bag of flour. Just divide by 10 or 20 when you're done.

Add your materials costs together and write that number at the bottom of the worksheet.

Materials

List the various materials and supplies that go into your product. If your items are small, think in batches and divide by the number of products in a batch.

Add everything together and write it at the bottom of the sheet.

_____ $ _____

_____ $ _____

_____ $ _____

_____ $ _____

_____ $ _____

_____ $ _____

_____ $ _____

Total materials per product: $ ☐

Labor

Labor can be estimated in a variety of ways – for example, you can use a stopwatch to time yourself and pay yourself an hourly rate, much like you would an employee. Or you can think of labor in blocks, more like a salary. How much would you like to get paid per day, week, or month? If you use the salary method, you'll need to do a bit of math to estimate how many products you could create in that same amount of time to create a "per product" amount.

Another way to estimate labor is to take a more intuitive approach: how much are your time and skills worth? How much would you like to be paid to make your product? This approach is about picking a number that feels right. If your product involves a high degree of skill or expertise, this method may more accurately capture those factors than an hourly rate. After all, in this scenario you're not just estimating the amount time it takes to make the item – you're estimating the value of your skills or expertise, which may vary from one product to another.

Because you can estimate labor in a variety of ways, there are several worksheets, each taking a different approach. Choose one and use it to estimate your labor for your product.

Labor: Hourly Method

The Hourly Method uses an hourly rate to calculate your labor. Use a clock or stopwatch to time yourself making your product. Decide on an hourly wage and multiply the two together.

Labor hours per product: _____

Hourly wage: $ _____

Multiply line 1 times line 2: [　　　　　]

Value of labor

Labor: Salary Method

The Salary Method uses a block of time to calculate labor costs. How much would you like to get paid per half day, full day, or week? How many products can you make during that same period of time?

Divide the your salary rate by the number of products you can create during that time.

How much would you like to
get paid per half day/day/week: $ _____

How many products you can
complete in the same amount   _____
of time:

Divide line 1 by line 2:

Value of labor

Labor: Intuitive Method

The Intuitive Method is all about estimating the value of your time and skills. It works best for products that require a high degree of skill or expertise.

What is the value of my time, skills, and expertise for this particular product?

Value of labor

Overhead

Overhead refers to any ongoing business expenses – basically any money you pay to keep your creative business up and running.

Overhead expenses are often called *indirect expenses* because they're necessary to keep the proverbial doors open, but aren't directly related to a specific product. Because of this, they can be tricky to quantify. But ideally, you'll want your price to offset a percentage of these expenses so your business is sustainable.

The best way to estimate overhead is to keep track of your ongoing business expenses for a period of time – a month, quarter, or year, if possible – and average it out. What do you pay on average per day, week, month, or quarter to keep your business running?

Include things like rent and utilities if you have a separate workspace, home office expenses if you work within a designated portion of your home, business taxes, insurance, credit card processing fees, website hosting, etc. Look around you as you work – what things other than materials and supplies do you pay for? Look back at your receipts for a period of time, or refer to a previous year's tax return.

As for how much of your overhead to include in your Price Box, the best way to determine this is to connect your product to a specific length of time. How many products could you make in a day or week? What would your overhead be for that same length of time? For example if you make ten items per week and spend an average of $100 per week on overhead, your estimate would be $100 per week divided by ten items per week = $10 per item.

The following worksheets will help you calculate your monthly overhead, then your overhead per product.

Monthly Overhead

Calculate your ongoing expenses for a single month.

Rent/Home office: $ _____

Utilities: $ _____

Business taxes: $ _____

Processing fees: $ _____

Other: _____ $ _____

Other: _____ $ _____

Total monthly overhead: $ [   ]

Overhead Per Product

Calculate your overhead for a single product.

Total monthly overhead
from previous worksheet: $ _____

Number of products
you can make per month: _____

Divide line 1 by line 2: $ _____
Overhead per product

Venue: Retail vs. Wholesale

The last few worksheets focused your product, but how and where you sell that product can have a big impact on its price. When it comes to venues, there are a variety of places you can sell your work, but they basically fall into one of two categories: *retail* and *wholesale*.

Retail means you're selling directly to the buying public. While you'll certainly incur some expenses while doing so, you're not sharing the "selling" part with anyone else. You're directly connecting to your customers with no one in between. You don't necessarily have to meet them face to face; someone could buy from your online shop or social media account and you'd never see them in person. But you know their name, what they bought, and where to send it.

Wholesale means there's a middleman involved. You're giving your product to someone else who's selling it to the end buyer. You're part of a larger buying chain, A to B to C. For our purposes, it doesn't much matter who or what the middleman is – if they're part of the process, they'll need to make a buck, just as you will. They'll have expenses, just as you do. And your final price, the one the end buyer pays, will be split amongst everyone involved.

Let's look at the specific arrangements you may have and how your price might be shared.

For the sake of easy math, let's say you have a product priced at $100. If you sell that product retail, you'll make the item and the customer will buy it – easy peasy. You'll hand them the item and they'll hand you the hundred bucks. There may be costs involved in selling that item – in addition to materials and labor, you may pay to rent a studio or storefront, pay for a website or online sales platform, or incur transaction fees when a buyer pays with a credit card. But those costs will be factored into your overhead.

If you sell your product wholesale, someone else does the selling for you. You put your work in a store that someone else owns, on a website that someone else runs, or in a catalog that someone else maintains. In exchange for their hard work, they get to earn an income as well as you. You either split that hundred bucks with them, or you sell them your product at a discount – say $50 instead of $100.

This is often referred to as *keystone pricing*, the "keystone" being the center stone of a bridge. It refers to the act of splitting the income right down the middle. There will still be costs involved – for both you and your middleman – but your costs (the overhead and labor involved in selling your work) are less because someone else is doing the selling for you.

Depending on your third party arrangement, you may not split the price tag evenly. Some venues do a 60/40 or 70/30 split, where you as the creator keep the larger portion. This is typical in consignment arrangements, where your work is put into someone else's shop and you don't get paid until it sells. This is commonly used for certain types of non-perishable creative items like artwork, clothing, or decor. You're essentially loaning your product to a third party with the understanding that you'll get paid once the end buyer purchases it.

If you're new to selling through a third party, a 50% discount (or even 40% or 30%) can be a large cost to swallow. How can someone who didn't even make the thing walk away with half your money??

But know that they're doing important work, just as you are. They deserve to be paid, just as you do. In addition to simply selling your work, they're providing access to their market, and maybe even giving you more consistent – or just plain *more* – sales.

The trick to managing a wholesale discount is simply to price your work appropriately for this sort of arrangement. If you're splitting the end price with a vendor (as in consignment), your price will need to absorb the discount. If you're discounting your items for a vendor (as in wholesale), your price will need to allow the vendor room to mark up your items enough to make a profit. They'll set the end retail price in this case.

To go back to the Price Box concept, if you'll be selling your work through a third party, you'll need to include those costs or accommodate that discount in your Price Box. Even if you only currently sell your work retail, if you plan to sell through a middleman in the future, leave room in your Price Box to fit those costs.

Price Box: Total Costs

On the following worksheet, add up your product's materials, labor, overhead, and venue expenses. Put the total you come up with into the Price Box on p. 70. Then, compare that number to your Market Price from p. 50.

Price Box: Total Costs

Write your product's materials, labor, and overhead costs below. Take these numbers from the previous worksheets. Add in any venue costs you incur selling your work.

Then, add everything together.

Materials per product (from p. 55): $ _____

Labor (from p. 57-59): $ _____

Overhead per product (from p. 63): $ _____

Venue expenses: $ _____

Total costs: $ [_____]
  Price Box

Price Box vs. Market Price

*Write your Price Box number in the box below.
Write your Market Price from p. 50 on the price tag.
Then, compare the two.*

If your Price Box is the slightly less than or the same as your Market Price, great! If not, read Putting It All Together and make adjustments.

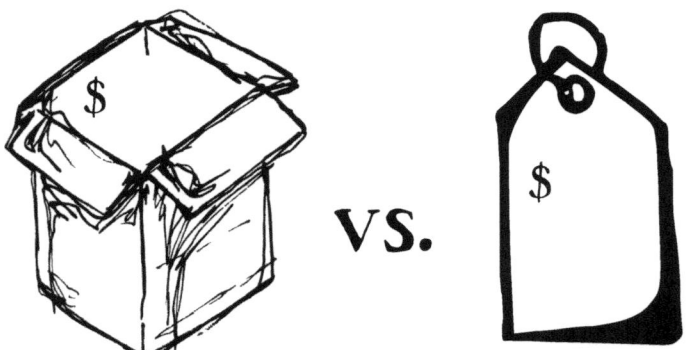

Price Box vs. Market Price Comparison

If everything fits in your Price Box, as in your costs are slightly less than or the same as your Market Price, great! That means your product costs about what the market expects to pay.

If your costs are much higher or lower than your Market Price, you'll need to do a bit of scrutinizing.

Take a look at these three areas in particular:

1. Double check your costs.

If your Price Box is higher than your Market Price, start by taking a close look at your costs. If you're early in your selling career, it's not uncommon to have higher costs than you ultimately will. You may be experimenting with a wider variety of materials, buying those materials in less cost effective quantities, working less efficiently than you will in the future, or have fewer sales to balance out your overhead.

If the above resonates, consider taking a little less in labor for a short time and focus on bringing down costs and streamlining your processes. Are there ways you can save time or money? Buy your materials at a discount? Work more efficiently? Batch your processes? Lower your overhead? If so, implement those adjustments as circumstances allow and you'll create a situation where you increasingly make more money over time.

If not...

2. Double check your market.

The other cause of a high Price Box/low Market Price mismatch is believing your work is more accessible than it truly is. This can range from placing your work at the lower end of your comps to being in a more exclusive market than you may realize.

Go back to your comps and take a closer look. Do you need to be at the higher end of the range? Is your product truly aligned with your market? Or is your product more exclusive than you originally thought? Adjust as necessary.

3. Make sure you're not missing a cost.

If your Price Box has a lot of room left over, make sure you're not missing or underestimating a major cost such as labor, overhead, or venue. For example, your Market Price may reflect a wholesale arrangement for your comps, but you're selling retail. That difference can be up to 50% of the price, or double your costs. In addition, make sure you're valuing your time and fully covering the labor involved in *selling* your work, not just creating it. But don't go below your Market Price in this situation unless you truly feel your work should be in a more accessible market.

Unless you find a major discrepancy here, a Price Box/Market Price mismatch is all about tweaking. It's like you're a chef cooking dinner adding a dash of this and a pinch of that until it's just right. Adjust until you feel comfortable, but then decide on a number and get out of the kitchen.

Your Right Price

The number you came up with is called your Right Price. It takes into account your product, your market, and your costs and expenses. Write it on the price tag on the following page.

Your Right Price

Write your Right Price on the price tag below.

Once you have this number, you can compare and contrast your product to any other similar items you sell. As long as the noun is the same, you can use your Right Price to determine the prices of similar goods based on a comparison of attributes. Sell *non-organic* hand-milled whole grain bread? Price it slightly less than the organic version. Sell a *family-sized* loaf? Price it higher than your standard loaf.

Pricing similar items is nothing more than tweaking the size of your Price Box based on its contents. If something takes more or less materials or time to make, quantify the difference. And then, do a gut check. Twice the materials *may* mean twice the price – but it also may not. If your packaging costs, labor, and overhead are the same, maybe 1.5 times the price feels more appropriate. As long as your starting price is solid, you can be intuitive here.

The Final Piece of the Puzzle

At this point there's only one thing standing between you and selling your work:

Confidence.

In the next chapter, I'll give you tips for building that confidence and getting comfortable communicating your price to buyers.

The Value of Work

The Value of Worth

You crunched a lot of numbers in the last chapter. But at the end of the day, price is meaningless if you aren't comfortable conveying it to potential buyers. In this chapter, we're going to talk about communicating your price – and what makes that sticky in the first place.

The difficulty with price comes when we assign value to our work, and by extension, ourselves. We assume the process will be cut and dry, like a math formula – but in reality, it can tap into a deep, emotional well. That's because when we put a number on something we create, we're often putting a value on our *worth*. And that can be sticky for a whole lot of reasons.

When you put your work out into the world, particularly when it's something you've lovingly created, price often has less to do with the perceived value of the product and more to do with the emotional aspects of selling.

If you think selling feels icky or sleazy and you want to stay firmly in the "nice" camp, you may undervalue your work or be quick to discount.

If you're afraid that if you price too high no one will buy your stuff and you'll feel like a failure, you may undercut your price to avoid feeling vulnerable.

If you don't feel confident putting your work out there, you may react to a lack of sales by backpedaling on your price, discounting, or second guessing yourself.

If you've had it drilled into you to charge what you're worth, you may look at what the pros are asking, put on your chutzpah, and overcharge for your products, not realizing all the invisible factors that went into their success. If it doesn't work, you may be left with an empty pocket and a head full of imposter syndrome.

Like I said, *sticky*.

When it comes to price, it's easy for people to say it's just business. But while that may be technically true, there are emotional factors that come into play whenever money is involved. These factors don't make you a bad person or less of a professional. In fact, they *make* you a person. A human being capable of feeling emotions, sensing nuance, and adapting to situations.

All of these are good qualities, and they're helpful when it comes to making your creative products. But they can work against you when it comes to factors involving money.

So what do you do about it?

The Value of Work

Start by acknowledging any pricing discomforts you may have. Then, use what you've learned throughout this book to create a counterweight. There are lots of factors that go into price including the various attributes of your product, your market, your costs, and your venue. You now know these factors well and have worked hard to quantify them. When you feel your emotional scales being tipped too far in an uncomfortable direction, counter it with a rational thought from the opposite side. Feel the scales come back into equilibrium.

In other words...

Shift your thoughts from the value of your <u>worth</u> to the value of your <u>work</u>.

This is an important way to take the ickiness out of talking about money. When you slide price from *person* to *product*, it naturally becomes more objective. You're just talking about a thing, and that thing has attributes. And those attributes have value – value your price conveys, and value your Right Buyer will be willing to pay for.

So what does this look like in practice?

If you're selling in person, it's all about active listening and observing body language. If you're selling online, you'll convey the same stories and information through your images, descriptions, and website.

When you see someone taking an interest in your product, tell them a story to further cultivate that interest. How was it made? What was your inspiration? What makes it unique?

When you see someone quietly contemplating your work, give them space to contemplate.

When you hear someone questioning your product or price, answer their questions. Convey the features, materials, or craft of your work.

When you sense someone reacting less positively to your price, respond with information that will help them connect that price to the value of your product. Once they understand the value your price represents, they may be willing to pay for it.

And if they aren't willing to pay for it, quietly say to yourself:

You are not my buyer.

Not every person is your customer in the same way not every person is your friend, your confidant, your spouse, or your partner. People are allowed to be browsers, onlookers, and tire kickers in the same way they're allowed to be acquaintances and strangers. Call them shopper acquaintances if it helps. Exchange a few pleasantries, then let them go about their day. Your Right Buyer will be the person who happily gives you money for your work.

Getting Ready For Market

As we wrap up this chapter, I want to send you off with a few price guidelines that will help you get your product ready for market. These are designed to help you take the *ick* out of talking about price.

1. Make your price visible.

Making your price visible does two things. One, it helps you avoid an uncomfortable conversation (i.e. talking about money). You don't have to talk about it if the customer doesn't have to ask! They simply see it on a price tag. And two, it makes your price feel more concrete, which facilitates buyer trust.

An added bonus: customers are less inclined to negotiate if they see your price in tangible form. Win-win!

2. Change your language.

If talking about money feels icky, talk about *budget* or *price point* instead. Budget doesn't pass judgement on how extravagant or cheap something is. Price point is simply a number. A simple shift in language can take the discomfort away.

3. Make your price consistent.

Unless you are wholesaling to a middleman, don't change your price from one buyer to the next, or from one venue to the next. This creates an environment that is unfair to both your buyers and venues.

While you may choose to discount your work (more on that in *Strategic Pricing: Coupons and Discounts*), be sure those discounts are offered to everyone rather than a single buyer asking for a favor.

When it comes to pricing, a great rule of thumb is:

While you can change your price over time, you should never change your price under pressure.

4. Raise your price, don't lower it.

Increase your price over time as your costs increase, or as your personal or professional situation changes. But aside from temporary discounts, don't decrease them. Trust the number you came up with, and let it grow with you. If you're just starting out and are unsure of your price, it's okay to lean toward the lower end of the spectrum. It may be more comfortable for you in the short term, and will give you room to grow in the future.

5. Commit to your market.

Your Right Buyer will be the one who values your work and is willing to pay for it. If your product, price, and market are aligned, your Right Buyer will find you. It may take time, but your patience will pay off – literally.

Strategic Pricing

Strategic Pricing is the advanced chapter of this book. It contains a variety of different pricing strategies designed to help you think more deeply about your personal and professional goals. Read through if you feel ready to take your creative business to the next level.

Note: you don't have to implement all of these. Choose those that resonate and do a dive deep, one at a time.

Tiered Pricing: Bread and Butter

As I mentioned in *The Three Markets*, it's possible, and often strategic, to offer products in more than one market. The key is not to mix markets for the *same* product. Let's talk about when it may make sense to sell your items in two markets and how to approach it.

Offering products in two different markets can add variety to your product line and build resiliency into your creative business. For example, if you typically sell to an exclusive market, offering a product or two at a midrange price point can give you a way to reach people who are not quite ready to pay a premium, or who want to test the waters with a less expensive item.

To create tiered price points, simply take a product you currently make and sell and add a simpler/less expensive or higher/more expensive version to your offerings. A good rule of thumb is a 1:5 or 1:10 ratio. For example, if you have a product that sells for $100, what could you offer for $10 or $20? Conversely, if your products are on the lower end of the scale, what could you offer for five or ten times the price?

An easy way to do this is to change the size or scope of your product: a piece of artwork becomes a less expensive print; a simple necklace becomes a showcase piece of jewelry. Another way is to create a bundle or collection: a whole grain loaf of bread might become a gift basket of assorted baked goods and spreads.

If those don't neatly apply to your product, read back through *Market Price: The Five Attributes*. What features or materials can you adjust to make a lower or higher end version of your item?

The lower priced items in these scenarios is sometimes referred to as your *bread and butter* work, because it often becomes an inventory staple. Many creative professionals find that they naturally sell more of their lower priced items. They don't make more *income* from those items – selling ten $10 items is the same revenue as one $100 item. But they tend to sell more.

There are two key factors in making a tiered pricing strategy effective: having similar products in each of the two markets, and reaching two adjacent markets. Having similar products – products where the noun is the same but the adjectives are different – is important because you're not building a customer base from scratch. People already know you and your product, this one is just slightly different.

Reaching two adjacent markets is important because there's naturally a bit of overlap between them – a person who normally buys your midrange item may splurge on a higher end product. Trying to span all three markets, or the lowest and the highest, is a recipe for brand confusion. Stick with a 1:5 or 1:10 bread and butter ratio and you'll do just fine.

Market Positioning: Price and Packaging

Market positioning is an important way to attract the right audience – we talked about this in *The Three Markets*. We'll dive a little deeper here.

Creative professionals sometimes mistakenly believe that a lower price point will be more attractive to buyers. This is not always the case, and with creative items in particular, it can be just the opposite. Having a price that is too low can subconsciously communicate that an item is cheap or less attractive.

Here's how it works.

When a product's quality is unknown, buyers take their cues from market positioning, which is made up of two primary elements: *price* and *packaging*. Which means if you're aiming to attract a higher end crowd, your price should reflect that. By nudging your price toward a higher market, you communicate the quality of your product and attract an audience that will appreciate it.

As a buyer, you intuitively understand the relationship between price and quality. If you go on a road trip and are looking for a bite to eat, you know instinctively that a $10 burger is going to be better than a 79 cent patty before you even walk in the door.

Your buyers know this, too. They look at your work and gauge its quality using context clues. And what are the two biggest context clues? You got it: *price* and *packaging*.

So why these two in particular?

Because they're the parts of your product your customer experiences *before* they buy. When your price and packaging are in agreement, i.e. a higher price and a classy box, your audience will assume your product is in agreement as well, i.e. a high quality item. When your price and packaging are not aligned, i.e. a higher price but a cheap display, your audience will have no clear way to gauge your item's quality – which can cause confusion at best, erode trust at worst, and lead to fewer sales.

This does not mean that a higher price automatically equals more sales. The key to making this technique work is to keep your price aligned with the quality and features of your product. In other words, use price and packaging to communicate the aspects of your product that a customer won't experience until *after* they buy.

Price as a Predictor

One of the most common ways to use price strategically is to create a formula for future offerings. Use it to price new products, price variations on current offerings, or quote a price for custom items – in other words, items where the noun is the same but the adjectives are different. This is easiest to do if you already have a new product in mind.

Start by determining which aspects of your original item stay consistent and which ones change – in other words, which aspects are *fixed* and which are *dynamic*. While it's possible that any aspect of your work could change, what you're looking for here are the variables that change in order to create the new item.

Let's start with the fixed variables.

Does your design time remain pretty much the same regardless of product? Do your materials costs tend to be consistent for work of a similar size? Do your overhead expenses tend to be consistent? What about packaging or customer service aspects? Think about things like prep, materials, time, labor, or any other factors specific to your work.

For example, a photographer may have the same setup regardless of whether their subject is a child or a newlywed couple. A dressmaker may take an hour to sew a particular garment regardless of fabric type. A woodworker may need a certain amount of lumber to make an item, regardless of what type of wood they use. A graphic designer may spend an afternoon designing a logo, regardless of what that logo will be for. That's not to say these factors can't or won't ever change, but for a similar product, their cost in terms of money or time tends to stay consistent. These are the *fixed* parts of your equation.

Next look at the factors which tend to vary. A photographer may have an extra expense if they travel to a wedding instead of shooting at their studio. A dressmaker may need time to source and buy new fabric for a special order. A woodworker may spend more money on an unusual species of wood than a common one. A graphic designer may need more time to prep a logo for print than for online use. These are the *dynamic* variables of your equation. As your product changes, these are the aspects that change along with it.

On the following worksheet, write down all of your product's variables. Arrange them roughly like an equation:

prep + materials + time + packaging = PRICE

Include anything that may be relevant to your product.

Draw a box around each of your fixed variables. Think of the box as encasing them in concrete. They aren't going to change. Or if they do change, they're not changing in a manner that impacts your time or expenses.

Draw a circle around your dynamic variables. Think of the circle as a balloon that can inflate or deflate – it can become larger or smaller depending on the circumstances.

As you price new products, compare them to your original product. What changes? By how much? Quantify the difference. For example if the size of your product doubles, maybe your materials balloon becomes twice as large. But other variables stay the same. A product that's twice as big may not need a price that is twice as large if the design time, communication, and packaging stay the same.

Do this for every similar product you sell. Once you get the hang of it, it becomes more intuitive. Just inflate the variables that change and quantify the difference.

Pricing New Items

*Write each of your original product's variables.
Arrange them like an equation:*

prep + materials + time + packaging = PRICE

Draw a box around each of your fixed variables, i.e. those that don't change from the original product to the new one.

*Draw a circle around your dynamic variables.
Think of the circle as a balloon that can inflate or deflate.
If a particular variable doubles, its circle becomes twice as big. Use this to estimate price for new offerings.*

Coupons And Discounts

While I don't believe in lowering prices for your products, if used judiciously, coupons and discounts may be one way to do so that keeps your integrity intact.

Coupons and discounts can work in a variety of ways. Sometimes we assume they work because of a supply and demand relationship, i.e. when price is lower, demand goes up. While that is sometimes the case, their real value is much more nuanced.

A coupon or discount may bridge a trust gap. When people buy from an unknown source, i.e. little ol' you, they may be hesitant at first. You're an unknown quantity. They need to trust you to not run off with their cash or credit card number, and trust that your items will be worth what they pay. A small discount may sweeten the deal enough to tip the scales in your favor.

Another way coupons and discounts entice buyers is by adding the element of urgency. If they can buy your item at any time, they may put it off until later. But if the coupon expires on a particular date, they now have a deadline to consider.

I personally prefer to offer discounts on selected bundles of items. This creates an incentive for someone who is already considering a single item to upgrade their purchase to several. Buyers who don't want the offer can easily opt out, but those who take advantage of it will be rewarded. It also means I'm not compromising on my item price – consistency is important.

Coupons and discounts can also work well as a way to reward loyal customers. If you have repeat buyers (or want to create some), they can be a great way to extend your thanks and deepen the creator/consumer relationship.

That said, discounts of any kind work best when they are used judiciously. Like any reward, if it is given too often, it becomes expected. You likely know this from your own buying habits. When you see a store constantly putting out 20% off coupons, you're more likely to wait for the next coupon instead of paying full price. You get conditioned to watch for the next ad. Use your discounts like a special treat and you won't be working against yourself.

Likewise, if you decide to discount your work in any way, be sure it fits into a larger marketing strategy. You don't want to constantly be rewarding new customers and neglecting your regular buyers. My local internet company does this – new buyers are given a whopping discount for the first six months. After that, the price goes up and the service goes down – not a great equation for happy long term customers.

Most importantly, be sure your price can absorb any discounts you offer. You don't want to go through the work of finding your Right Price only to give money away in the form of a coupon or discount. If a discount gives you an opportunity to more quickly entice new buyers, or increases the value of returning customers, then the time it saves you in marketing may be worth the cost. If not, it may not be the right tool for you.

Pricing for Personal and Professional Growth

You may have noticed throughout this book that I didn't mention the concept of *profit*. That was intentional. As a micro creative business, profit is kind of a squishy concept. Let's dive into it here.

First, let's look at profit in the context of a big business.

My husband works for a large company. Their expenses include the labor of their employees, the materials costs connected to the services they provide, and the overhead costs related to keeping the lights on and machinery running.

And profit? It's four cents on every dollar they aim to make above and beyond everything else.

Now, let's look at a micro creative business.

Let's say you're a baker. Your expenses include your labor, the materials costs of the breads you bake, and the overhead costs related to keeping the lights on and oven running.

But profit? It isn't any of those. At best, just like a larger company, it's a few cents on the dollar above and beyond your other expenses.

Stated more clearly,

The money you make from your labor is not profit.

Imagine for a moment you hired someone to do your job. You'd pay them wages for their labor. Since you were no longer doing the work, you wouldn't get paid those same wages. Profit is what your business earns *after* those wages.

Most of the time, this distinction doesn't matter. What difference does it make whether the money is wages or profit? It all spends the same.

But it matters when it comes to growing your business. Growth often takes money – you may need to invest in your space or upgrade your equipment. Or, you may need to invest in yourself by taking a class or hiring a coach to expand your skills or knowledge.

But where does that money come from?

In a micro creative business, we often initially use the income we would otherwise pay ourselves to grow our business. In the early days of start up, this is normal – a business needs funds to get established and take hold.

But long term, you need a more sustainable source of funds.

So how do you reinvest in your business?

You use what I call *pricing for personal and professional growth*.

I wrote about buying a house in *Market Price*, but when my husband and I were buying our farm, our decision involved much more than just money. Our personal preferences came into play. Our long-term goals. Our vision for the future. The same is true with your creative work.

Price decisions are rarely only about money. Sure, you want to sell your work. But you're selling it for a reason. You have bigger goals in mind.

Maybe you want to build a nest egg so you can quit your day job. Maybe you need a new piece of equipment so you can work more efficiently. Maybe you want to invest in a bigger space. Maybe you want to donate a portion of your revenue to charity.

Think about your long term goals. Is there one you'd like to work toward? Give it a dollar amount and a time frame. And then, do a bit of math. How many products would you have to sell per day, week, or month over a period of time to get there?

The key here is to quantify your goals in concrete numbers. Our brains work best when they have something specific to work toward. Better yet, make your goal visual. Track your progress in a visible way. You're more likely to stay motivated while working toward your goal when you can see progress, whether that's setting up a separate bank account or coloring in a chart on your wall. Small amounts add up over time, and you'll literally see it occur.

I mentioned pricing formulas at the beginning of this book, and here's where they truly fall flat. Formulas that focus only on time and materials leave out the most important part of the equation: *you*.

You're allowed to have long term goals. You're allowed to work toward something bigger than yourself.

And your price is allowed to reflect that. So long as you're within the range of your Market Price, add a little space to your Price Box to fit your dreams.

Thank you for reading!

I hope you've enjoyed this book, and I wish you all the best on your creative journey! If you need someone to help you navigate that journey, send me an email at:

Chris@MakeSomethingMeaningful.org

or go to MakeSomethingMeaningful.org to see our full collection of books and resources.

Take care,

Chris

www.ingramcontent.com/pod-product-compliance
Lightning Source LLC
Chambersburg PA
CBHW042026100526
44587CB00029B/4316